All Of My Life
Devotional

Lorie-Ann Brown

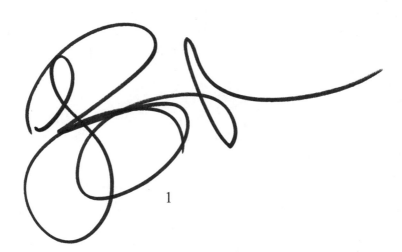

All Of My Life
Devotional

ISBN: 978-1-64921-172-9

Published By: Kelly Publishing 2020

All Of My Life
Devotional

All Of My Life
Devotional

Table of Contents

All Of My Life
Devotional

Dedication

I dedicate this book to the work of God in every
individual's life. God has a purpose He strongly desires to
fulfill in all of us and I strongly believe each word printed
on these pages, are drenched in the life-changing, life-
fixing blood of Jesus. I recommend as you read, you read
slowly and savor each word God is speaking to you.

Acknowledgments

I thank God, first and foremost for speaking to me and through me to produce His work.

I thank Apostle Samuel Fatoki, for giving me the opportunity of a lifetime to start an assignment that was long overdue. God used you to propel me forward into His will and timing.

I thank Prophetess Marcia Fatoki for continually speaking in and over my life and encouraging me gently to be strong in the Lord and pursue the greatness He has embedded in me. You are indeed a true woman of God!

I thank my beloved sister, Nickesha Morris, for always believing I can, even when I say I can't. You have been a true confidant and encouragement in times I needed it most.

I thank Prophetess Kelly Crews of Kelly Publishing from the bottom of my heart for following the leading of Christ and taking on the task of making this book possible to the world.

And last but not least, I thank my parents, Lillian and Eric Brown, for a lifetime of encouragement, teachings and training. You have encouraged me of the greatness that lies in me, even when I did not have eyes to see it.

2020 The Year Of The Supernatural

What has been and what could've been does not compare to what is to come. Welcome to 2020!!

We have crossed over into divine spiritual vision, supernatural favor, a year of rest through divine establishment, 2020 vision and so much more of what God has spoken over this year to each of us corporately and individually. As you reminisce on the things of 2019 and create goals for 2020, are you aligned to receive what the Lord has spoken over this new chapter?

Let us align ourselves to receive all the Lord has promised us in this year spiritually and naturally. It is our inheritance to walk in the authority of Christ, to live like Kingdom citizens where we lack no good thing. It is our charge to walk upright and serve the Lord with all He has blessed us with.

In this year 2020, let us align ourselves to the plans of God for our life and generation. Let's hide under his covering and know that He is God and He will never leave us nor forsake us. Let us accept God's promises as they leave His lips, live in the manifestations and increase the Kingdom of God here on earth. Let's let our lights shine in this new decade that men may see our good works, our supernatural favor and inquire of the God we serve.

Happy New Year to one and all!

Appointment With Destiny

The Lord showed and gave an analogy of what unforgiveness can be described as and of course, it can have many different depictions, but this one stood out. It was a nice, healthy, pink heart beating, then a small black spot appears on it, which begins to spread until the entire human heart is black. As it's spreading, the Spirit of God begins to move away and is blocked. As the Lord showed the heart covered in unforgiveness, He showed His space is also taken up.

Saints, it's beneficial to our individual souls to forgive. It's beneficial to our physical health to forgive. It's beneficial to our eternal destiny to forgive. It's beneficial to our spiritual health to forgive. It's beneficial to our financial peace to forgive. It's beneficial to our relationship with God to forgive others and even our own selves.

Today, I want us to focus a bit on forgiving ourselves. We sometimes become so upset with our own selves that we punish ourselves from trying again, taking another risk, continue kicking ourselves, all because we tried and failed, or even tried scared and still failed. But, do you know that failure isn't final, but rather educational?

To forgive yourself requires compassion, empathy, accepting responsibility, knowing that God does not waste mistakes, stopping rumination (it's done and past, so it can be let go of), learning from it, stopping condemning voices and welcoming the peace of God and peace with God, back in your life (1 Peter 5:7). As you do this and more, a heart once black will become healthy once more and the presence of God can continue to fully function in your lives. Remember, our imperfections prove how much we need God, and our mistakes are opportunities for Him to increase us further in wisdom.

You are not condemned; you are not a failure and you are more than a setback (Romans 8:28 & 37). Allow the greatest helper, the Holy Spirit, to teach you how to forgive yourself for all the past mistakes you've held on to and the present ones you can't seem to walk past.

Prayer

Heavenly Father, I thank You for the opportunity to let my request be known unto You and to cast all my cares on You. Lord Jesus, I know You care for me and Your love for me is far greater than any mistake I can make. You know the plans You have for me are good, to give me a prosperous future and an expected end. Lord, I know every tomorrow is my prosperous future and no mistake will hold me down. Lord, as You command to forgive and be forgiven, I forgive myself for all mistakes I have held myself accountable to for far too long, things I had no control over and things I could not change; I release myself. I forgive myself for allowing condemnation and the lies of the enemy to dictate my identity and purpose; I release myself. Lord, I now walk in liberty, knowing that You have forgiven me and will now restore unto me the wisdom needed to go forward.
In Jesus' name, I pray, amen!

My Declaration

_____
_____
_____
_____
_____
_____
_____
_____
_____
_____
_____
_____
_____
_____
_____
_____
_____
_____
_____
_____
_____
_____
_____
_____
_____

All Or Nothing

When we read the scriptures, we can sometimes become lost in the "how do I really do this" and/or "is that even still possible?". We know that faith is the currency of heaven which moves God to act on your behalf, but what do we do when we are being tested. When a situation or circumstance hits where the faith you know, the mustard seed kind is not enough anymore; what do you do. Do you throw in the towel, settle for less or scream at God in regret and dismay? Beloved, you pray for the gift of Faith...the faith that allows you to wholly lay your life on the line knowing that based on the mere fact that you no longer exist in shifting that particular situation, God is able to fully take over. We can, at times, face situations that push us over the edge to where we do not know what to do anymore. This is the perfect recipe to see God work, for, in this, we no longer have control.

God is moved by faith! When we do this, I can imagine God is ecstatic to stretch us beyond our capacity in order to both answer the huge (in our eyes) request we prayed for and then prove more than we can ever bargain for. It is rather exciting if you allow yourself to think about it! Imagine being on human faith street and God pushes you to the gift of faith boulevard. Oh, the possibilities!!! Oh, the impossibilities to die, doubts being annihilated and our faith in God abounding more and more (2 Corinthians 2:8-7).

On this road, we can go back and pray for those prayers we once prayed and was never answered because faith was lacking, and watch the Gift of faith, now in our enlarged capacity, manifest them! So exciting!

Prayer

Lord, I thank You for the gift of faith. I thank You that what was once impossible in my eyes, I now see possible through Your eyes. Thank You for the manifestations as I allow You to have Your way in my life, by faith. Take all of me, Lord and have Your way. In Jesus' name, amen!

My Declaration

_____
_____
_____
_____
_____
_____
_____
_____
_____
_____
_____
_____
_____
_____
_____
_____
_____
_____
_____
_____
_____
_____
_____
_____
_____
_____
_____
_____
_____
_____

Are We Truly Sold Out?

"I'm sold out completely to God" is a very famous statement in the body of Christ. But what does it mean to be completely sold out? Does it mean we try our best daily to be as good as we can be? Or when it is convenient for us, do we honor God? Or when things are going our way, or does it mean we honor, walk in true holiness even if our bed is at the side of the road for a season? The Word of God states, "By their fruits, you shall know them (Matthew 7:16-17,20)." It also said we all are to take up our cross and follow Christ (Matthew 16:24). So, are we truly sold out or are we living a passed down tradition, an obligation or a life we chose to live such as marriage, where we vow to honor in all things "till death do we meet our Savior face to face?"

We are here in this life, but for a time, then are gone as vapor with the wind. A sold-out life exemplifies not only that of Christ, but the Disciples and many men and women of our century, such as Lee Stoneking, William J. Seymour or Kathryn Kuhlman, who will and have honored God even to their deaths. Apostle Paul considered death a gain in the Kingdom of God (Philippians 1:21). He also exemplified "sold-out." To say these words out loud are not only hard prematurely, but frightening. But when one is "sold-out" and knows with all certainty that to live is Christ and to die is gain (Philippians 1:21), then we begin to live a life that continuously honors God, His Word and His standards.

One that seeks to please the Father and accept holiness, one that stands firm in the face of adversity knowing that light afflictions will come, but it is all worth it but for the glory of Christ!

Prayer

Father, You have created the earth and man with a purpose. You have replenished the fields and purified many hearts. Father, You have made the uncomely pleasant and loved even the worst of us. Lord, You have shown me in many examples what it truly means to be "sold-out" to You and that I desire Lord. If there is anything in me that has caused shame to Your name, I ask You to reveal it, I repent and ask You to forgive me so that I may live a life full of You, one that will never be on pause, a life of holiness. God, I surrender my all to You this day. Your will be done as I seek to be solely Yours. In Jesus' name, I pray, amen!

My Declaration

_____
_____
_____
_____
_____
_____
_____
_____
_____
_____
_____
_____
_____
_____
_____
_____
_____
_____
_____
_____
_____
_____
_____
_____

Chosen Bride
Unfailing Love

Hallowed be the name of the Lord in all the earth. As we honor God this day, let's remember all His benefits towards us. Life can become so busy that we forget why we truly exist; to be His glory carriers and to continually worship Him.

We were created as the bride of Christ; His church and like every bride, there is a groom...Jesus Christ!
Let's look at this love story: A man saw that His son needed a bride, so He went out and found the most beautiful one for him. However, the son had to prove His sincere love and pay a dowry for his bride. The bride also had to receive and reciprocate the love the groom comes giving in order for the relationship to flourish. So, the son/father gave up their most prized possession as a sacrifice to prove his love for the bride. But unfortunately, the bride in her imperfection would not comprehend or accept why such a huge sacrifice was made just for her; this was a grand gesture, but the son would not relent...he loved this bride.

Adam was created, but God the Father said, it was not good for him to be alone and gave him Eve, a bride. The earth was without void and form, Jesus was present, but it also was not good for Him to be alone, so God created the church to love Him exceedingly in our imperfections. Gomer left Hosea and went "a whoring," but the Lord sent him to retrieve her. Hosea did not comprehend it, but he obeyed. Gomer was taken out of bondage, brought to light, produced fruits, but her mindset wasn't changed, so she ended up in bondage again. God sent Hosea to purchase her once more—(Hosea 1, Hosea 3). We can use this story of God's love for us, His unconditional love that no matter where we are, how we are or what we are, He will always desire us. God sees our ending, or meaningfulness and not our present obstructive view that we may have. He sees our entire life with Him in it. What's not to love?

Do you love Him today? Knowing that He voluntarily chose you and stuck by you even when you rejected Him and ran the other way. What love is this that a man will lay down his life for a friend (John 15:3); self-sacrificial love. The love of God is truly reckless. By telling Hosea to buy back Gomer, after she unwittingly proved she wasn't worth love, He showed us that no matter how far we may roam, His love remains relentless, far-reaching and He chooses us daily.

Thank You, Jesus!!!!

My Declaration

Do You Truly Know God?

We quote scriptures. We sing songs. We perform in church, but one would ask, do we really know God? Do you truly know His unfailing love, His unwavering nature towards us? Do you know that God keeps His words, His promises, His decrees and declaration?

Beloved, do you know that He watches over you each night you slumber in sleep, unaware if someone is trying to break in your home or if the enemy is seeking to destroy you at your most vulnerable point! Do you know that He sends His angels to guard you and the vehicle you travel in daily with a hedge of protection? He is protecting you, right now, as you read this. Do you know that He can cause you to set things in order because He knows the end from the beginning? Do you know He has your entire life in His hands and all it requires is your surrendered will? Do you know the God you serve today?

The songwriter says God is a good good Father. He is one who corrects those He loves (Proverbs 3:11-12). He is one who never condemns, who picks us up when we fall, who forgives our sins when we ask, who provides for us in times of need, who wipes away our tears and mends our broken hearts. He is the one who causes us to walk boldly in our faith, knowing He has our backs. He is the one who causes us to trample on serpents and scorpions and the one who shuts the mouth of vipers and evil words against you. He is the one who causes your feet to be like hinds' feet to walk on high places (Habakkuk 3:19).

Do you truly know Him today?

He is our Jehovah Jireh
(The Lord will provide).
He is our El Elyon
(The Most High God; Psalm 57:2).
He is Jehovah Rapha
(The Lord that heals; Exodus 15:26).
He is El Olam
(Everlasting God; Genesis 21:33).
He is Jehovah Mekoddishkem
(The Lord who sanctifies you; Exodus 31:13).
He is Jehovah Nissi
(The Lord my banner; Exodus 17:15).
He is Jehovah-Raah
(The Lord my Shepherd; Psalm 23:1).
He is Jehovah Shammah
(The Lord is There; Ezekiel 48:35).
He is Jehovah Shalom
(The Lord Is Peace; Judges 6:24).
He is Jehovah Sabaoth
(The Lord of Hosts; 1 Samuel 1:3).
He is Jehovah Metsudhathi
(The Lord my High tower, Psalm 18:2).
He is Jehovah Ori
(The Lord my Light; Psalm 27:1).
He is Jehovah Sal'I
(The Lord my Rock; Psalm 18:22).
He is Immanuel
(God with us; Isaiah 7:14)
He is Elohim
(God; Genesis 1:1).

There are so many other names, but I will stop there.
Our God is great and bigger than everything we may face
in this life. He provides the faith and strength we need to
press through any difficult circumstances. He battles
anxieties (fear of future), and worries (present fears). Stand
on your rock (El Sali; 2 Sam 22:47) today and align with
the Holy Spirit in whatever situation you are facing.
Rejoice!! The victory is already yours!!

Be blessed!

My Declaration

_____
_____
_____
_____
_____
_____
_____
_____
_____
_____
_____
_____
_____
_____
_____
_____
_____
_____
_____
_____
_____
_____
_____
_____
_____
_____
_____
_____
_____

Equip Yourself

To do war, to do battle is the question. What lies in your possession that is worth fighting for? Is it your earthly possessions, family, friends or your soul? The things of the Spirit maybe....

The Lord desires for us to seek after Him for who He is and to fight for our soul as much as He does for us daily. Daily, we wake in life to a new day that we have never seen before and will never see again once it's gone. It's a new day.

Are you equipped to fight for your soul? Do we understand that our adversary cares nothing about our earthly possessions, but seeks to destroy us at the soul level, permanently?

It's time to go on the offense. Too long have we stayed in the defense awaiting attacks before we move. Let's put on the whole armor of God and fight the good fight of faith (Ephesians 6:11-18). Put on the helmet of salvation to fight out negative thoughts and circumstances with the powerful "Greater is He that is in me than He that is in the world." Let's throw swords of fire, knowing we CAN do all things through Christ, who strengthens us. Girt our loins with He shall never leave us nor forsake us. Use the shield of faith to cast down every dart and imagination that seeks to exalt itself above God and every worry. Hold up the breastplate of righteousness to be holy as He is holy, and keep your feet prepped with the gospel as we become peaceable with all men (Romans 12:18).

Let us be equipped and ready to defend the promises of God over us, His kingdom citizens. Sometimes, we give the enemy too much credit. He is unimportant, minuscule and of non-effect when God is for us. Who/what are we fighting for? Let our election be sure, today, as we partner with Jesus Christ in the battle towards victory!

Be thou strengthened with all might!!

Prayer

Heavenly Father, I thank You that I am a new creation. Old things are passed away and behold I am become new. Lord, I now forget the things of old that have hindered me from walking in the fullness of you. I release myself from every bitterness, anger, offense, pride, and unrighteousness and I take on Your identity. In You, I live and move and have my being. In You, I produce fruits. In You, I prosper. In You, I remain victorious. I put on the whole armor of God to stand against the wiles of the enemy and with You, my soul is intact. I bless Your name for Your covering and protection. In Jesus' name, amen.

My Declaration

_____
_____
_____
_____
_____
_____
_____
_____
_____
_____
_____
_____
_____
_____
_____
_____
_____
_____
_____
_____
_____
_____
_____
_____
_____
_____
_____
_____
_____

Hold On

What a lesson learned when we thought a thing once impossible becomes a reality in our life. How wonderful is our God that He doesn't mind taking us through the process of crushing and beating to get results out of us.
He takes time to perfect that which He calls blessed. He doesn't name a thing without bringing that purpose forward. So when life gets happy, rejoice in that season. When you face transitioning, hang on to God's unchanging hands to see you through and when life gets rough, hold out firmly on His Word for His promises never fail.

One thing about this God we serve is He has to abide by His word. Find your promise of Goshen, in your hard season and remember the promised land is but so far away. For in this land of the living, you will reap the rewards, if you faint not.

Trust His words today. Hold on to the promises of God as they will manifest in time.

My Declaration

He Has His Hands On You

Hymns, songs, and psalms can truly speak to our souls and circumstances. In this time, you may be facing some hard obstacles, but be encouraged beloved, the Lord is announcing today to heaven and hell that He has His hands on you. There is no "mountain" too high, no "valley" too deep, no impossible situation that God can't fix. He is the cure for cancer, the remediator to a custody battle, the judge in the courtroom, the final say when the odds are against you and I, and has the final authority over our lives.

The Lord said He will never leave nor forsake His children (Hebrews 13:5). He is the problem solver, the Holy Spirit, our comforter (John 14:26), and El Shaddai, our peace and our epitome of righteousness. All you may be feeling today, carry it to Him and leave it at His feet. Allow yourself to cast your burden on Him. Allow yourself to prove Him with the impossible. Yes, prove Him today. He is waiting on the edge of His seat for you to let Him have what you consider hard or impossible.

Open arms are one of the greatest acts of wisdom; wisdom to know you can't do this life on your own. Wisdom to know where you end and where God starts.

Prayer

Dear heavenly Father, how gracious and wonderful is Your name. I have proven You time and time again and Your track record remains faithful. Lord Jesus, I repent for allowing myself to worry and fret and for giving up at times. Lord, You created me strong and bold as I reside in You and You in me. Holy Spirit, I accept You as my comforter, my sound mind, and I release all my impossible situations to You today. I know You will carry my burdens. Your Kingdom come, Your will be done in my life. In Jesus' name, amen!

My Declaration

_____
_____
_____
_____
_____
_____
_____
_____
_____
_____
_____
_____
_____
_____
_____
_____
_____
_____
_____
_____
_____
_____
_____
_____
_____
_____
_____

Humility Is What It Takes

Being falsely accused, persecuted, spat on and more would cause anyone to retaliate. Throughout Jesus' ministry, we see the vilest things being said about Him, to Him and done to Him, but His humility increased. Jesus knew who He was and what His purpose in this life was. He refused to let anyone pull Him out of that "space." He kept His composure, said what He needed to say and fulfilled His purpose on earth.

Humility is key in maintaining a kingdom citizen's integrity and letting our light shine before men. The world needs to see something they do not possess. They need to desire what we have as children of God, which is humility, love, patience, temperance and all the other fruit of the Spirit.

As any parent desires for their child/children to represent them in the best way, our Lord and Savior Jesus Christ is no different. He wants us to represent Him in speech, modality, temperance, honesty, humility, holiness and integrity. Yes, sometimes situations will abound over all of this, but *quickly* get back to the nature God has called you to be in- *humility*.

A message was preached about what it takes to receive the things of God, and on that list was humility. Matthew 15:21-28 spoke about the woman of Canaan, who wasn't particularly appreciated by the disciples and ignored at first by Jesus because her season of redemption or salvation was not yet. The woman, although persistent, unashamedly humbled herself before Jesus even when he called her a dog. She could've walked away, felt disrespected, told him off, but she knew she was in the presence of greatness and she had an impossible request. Her humility was also wrapped with faith, which caused her to receive her blessings before time.

The character of a man or woman of God is vital in this season. We must glow Christ. We must think like Christ and have a conduct that is holy and acceptable unto God. This order was not given because we can obtain it within ourselves, Christ knows we must depend on Him to achieve His Kingdom and the things of it.

Prayer

Lord Jesus, I thank You for Your humility all the way to the cross. I thank You for the example You have laid out in Your word of how I, a child, an extension of You is to live a life that is firstly pleasing to You. Lord, I ask this day that You teach me how to be humble, teach me how to love my enemies, teach me how a soft answer will turn away wrath and teach me how to not be lovers of this world, but a lover of the Kingdom, in Jesus' name, amen.

My Declaration

_____
_____
_____
_____
_____
_____
_____
_____
_____
_____
_____
_____
_____
_____
_____
_____
_____
_____
_____
_____
_____
_____
_____
_____
_____
_____
_____
_____

The Joy Of The Lord

When the enemy comes in like a flood, our Lord and Savior raises a standard against him (Isaiah 59:19). The joy of the Lord is our strength (Nehemiah 8:10c). When our cups overflow with joy, we can't do anything but bask in the greatness of our Jehovah. When you think of God's mercy and grace, does it bring you to the point of deeper surrender and deeper consecration? We serve a purposeful God in that whatever He does, it is to produce something in us or to remove something out of us.

God deposits His joy in our being when we call on Him in times of deep distress or when He knows the pain we feel is just too much for our tiny hearts to bare or when He just wants us to smile. He carries us in His arms and protects us from seen and unseen dangers. I once heard a preacher say, "For many reasons we are children of God and not adults of God." This statement resounds true as we will forever need Him. Being a child puts us in a place of complete dependence, a place where we run to Daddy and He rescues us because we are His children and are unable to do life on our own.

As His children, He desires for us to be joyful, whole and dependent on Him. God cherishes our smiles and laughs. Sometimes, we, as children of God, do not realize how important we are to our Father. We were created to be His joy piece. The creation He looks on and smiles from His heart.

The one He made better than the angels (Hebrews 1:4-6); we even puzzle the angels (1 Peter 1:12). Our Daddy wants good things for us. He wants us to prosper in all we do, conquer in every conquest and endure in all good and needed things.

What love the Father has lavished us with. Allow yourself to stay under the joy of the Lord today. Also, jot down 5 ways the Lord has increased your joy or strength in difficult times. Allow the Holy Spirit to minister to you this day as you take inventory of His greatness.

My Declaration

Jehovah Jireh Sees Your Need

Have you taken some time lately and looked back on some then impossible situations that God took you out of? There were somethings that would've wrecked you, had they gone in the opposite direction. Jehovah Jireh is our ultimate help when our back is against the wall. When anxiety and fear seem to be winning, just call on Him. When you face another difficult situation, remember what He did for you before. Make it personal.

The Psalmist David said in Psalm 143:5, "I remember the days of old; I meditate on all thy works; I muse on the work of thy hands." David knew that keeping or remembering what God has accomplished prior would strengthen him in the present and future troubles. He knew that when death came for him, he would remember how God delivered his people from its hands. He knew that when sickness would toil in his body that God, his deliverer was just a prayer away. He knew that when he was lacking, he would not be a cast away because he kept his trust in God and based on past experiences, GOD WILL PROVIDE.

We do know that our afflictions are many, but we also know that we ARE delivered from ALL (Psalm 34:19). Push. Cast. Throw vehemently all your burdens, needs, difficult situations on God today. Do not carry it an inch further. At times, we get in the way of our own breakthroughs by trying to fix it. Don't fix it. You can't. Give it to Jehovah Jireh.

Prayer

Jehovah Jireh, I thank You for always giving me victory. I thank You for looking beyond my faults and recognizing my needs. As it says in your word Lord, You will supply all my needs according to Your riches, not mine, in glory. So, I thank You today for maintaining Your perfect track record and doing it again. I lay my needs by name (name your needs) before You this day and I cast them vehemently at Your feet. Surprise me once again, Lord. In Jesus' name, amen!

My Declaration

_____
_____
_____
_____
_____
_____
_____
_____
_____
_____
_____
_____
_____
_____
_____
_____
_____
_____
_____
_____
_____
_____
_____
_____
_____
_____

Let This Mind Be In You

We have often heard that the mind is a powerful tool. We have also heard that our adversary, satan, focuses on destroying us from that position, and this is true. The word of God advises us to think on the good, just, pure and righteous things in life (Philippians 4:8). This was no accident. The Lord knows that whatsoever we meditate on, whether consciously or unconsciously, we become (Proverbs 23:7). The word of God also commands that we love the Lord our God with all our heart, all our soul and all our mind (Matthew 22:37). Imagine who we will become when we allow ourselves to love our King, Master and Lord the way He commanded us.

Instead of diving into the exegesis of these scriptures, let's focus this devotion on the power we carry but do not utilize. Too often, we allow our minds to control us, thinking it has the final say or is always from God. Do not be deceived. Our minds really do play tricks on us and can get us into serious trouble with both man and God. If a child of God believes their life is limited, they will without a shadow of a doubt refrain themselves unequivocally from stepping out in growth, new adventures and pass up prominent opportunities. Why? Their mind controls their body and decisions and God's purpose is unable to be fulfilled in their lives.

Whatever we meditate on, we are bound to (Psalm 101:3). Think about it. If we meditate on not getting out of a particular situation, our lives will manifest worry and unbelief because now in our mind, "there is no way out." If we are wayward in decision makings, confusion now becomes our daily bread, instead of the Bread of Life. If we do not think things through, our whole rationale for life becomes skewed and impulse-driven. What does God say about our mind? What does He want to utilize it for?

Knowing that our mind is a powerful tool and can cause destruction in the wrong hands, we ought to carefully think, process and rely on God for every step we desire to take. Our minds can have biases, fears, regrets, resentments or today, we can CHANGE our minds. Yes, it is that simple to contain love, the Word of God, patience and allow God to renew it daily (Romans 12:2). When we change our minds from the world and shift it to God, we experience peace in our thought-life, we are no longer plagued with anxiety, and we sleep restful (Psalm 127:2). Another way to "change" our mind is to cast down every vain imagination or thought that seeks to make obscure and taint the character of Christ and our purpose in Him (2 Corinthians 10:5). By doing this, we will be able to think carefully, make decisions better and continually experience the peace and leading of God.

We are also to guard our minds against negative influences in the world, such as certain things we watch on TV, the music we listen to and conversations we have (Psalm 101:3; 1 Corinthians 15:33). We are also to pay close attention to those random thoughts that come to humiliate and make of non-effect the righteousness that God has placed upon us.

Let's renew our minds in Christ today (Romans 12:2). As we allow God to renew our minds, we transform our lives into one that Christ is free to use. We will carry a mind literally stayed on God and free from the shackles of this world. Let this mind be in you, which was also in Christ Jesus (Philippians 2:5).

Prayer

Heavenly Father, I thank you that I am a new creation and possess a brand-new mind, one tailored specifically and intentionally by You. You said in Your word, by faith, to speak those things that are not as though they are, and I speak life, peace, and purity over my mind this day and for the rest of my life. I ask You to help my mind and my life to be transformed by You. Let not vain imaginations, fret, fear or offense no longer control my thought process. Let all filthiness, immorality, wild thoughts, lewdness, arrogance and all things unrighteous be subjected right now under the obedience of Jesus Christ. I declare from this day forward, my mind will be a house for the Holy Spirit to commune and my mind will be that of Christ's. It will be filled with peace and continually available to hear the voice of God. Father, God, may Your peace that surpasses all understanding rest in my thought life and may You alone get the glory and full control over my mind. In Jesus' name, I pray, amen!

My Declaration

_____
_____
_____
_____
_____
_____
_____
_____
_____
_____
_____
_____
_____
_____
_____
_____
_____
_____
_____
_____
_____
_____
_____
_____
_____
_____
_____

Peace In Him

Let's look at this scripture for our devotion today. "The blessings of the Lord makes rich and adds no sorrow to it" (Proverbs 10:22). This scripture always comforts me in a time of transition and decision making. It is wonderful to know that whatever the Lord has predestined for me will bring me peace, joy and is enough to recognize the will of the Father. When we embark on a new journey, are transitioning whether for job, work, ministry and relationships, we should consider this scripture and test it. Is what you are embarking on bringing you peace or are you constantly stumbling between different opinions? Are you confused and can't make your mind up? We must remember that our Father is not the author of confusion (1 Corinthians 14:33), but one that delights in clarity. So, when we can't make up our minds, it's either our own fault in leaning to our own understanding or our adversary, the spirit of confusion.

Beloved, when the Lord gives good gifts or directions, there is always peace with it. When His approval is on our decision making, it comes final and with little, if any, back and forth (in our humanness). He truly adds no sorrow. This isn't to say we do not face some complications, but do not expect it! Allow God's peace to overshadow every confusion and doubt. Allow Him to take away what is not good and replace it with what you need. His good gifts come with righteousness, peace and joy.

Prayer

Heavenly Father, I thank You that You are not the author of confusion, but rather peace and clarity. Every situation and decision making that I've been battling with I give it to You this day, in Jesus' name. Lord, I ask You to lead me in the path of righteousness as I now stand in Your grace, allowing your peace to direct me. I release all discomfort, double-mindedness and confusion to You, In Jesus' mighty name, amen!

My Declaration

_____
_____
_____
_____
_____
_____
_____
_____
_____
_____
_____
_____
_____
_____
_____
_____
_____
_____
_____
_____
_____
_____
_____
_____
_____
_____
_____
_____
_____

Procrastination, The Thief

In prayer, I asked the Lord what He would like to speak to His people about and to my surprise, it was procrastination.

It's easy to put off for tomorrow what can be done today, but how beneficial is procrastination to our natural and spiritual being. That clutter in the corner that you have been passing for days keeps getting bigger and the time you keep missing to put aside to read or pray moves from days to weeks to months. And oh, how quickly it can pile up! When we are consumed with many tasks sometimes, we look, get discouraged, say we are too tired, too hungry or "I'll deal with it another day." Well, beloved, the day comes, and it's put off yet again.

The Lord has spoken to me on some occasions of laziness, asking, "Why put off for tomorrow what can be done today?" Each time I would hear Him say this, I wasn't fond of hearing it, but I knew it means that I need to take action immediately, so I would rise from slothfulness and do what needed to be done. Days would past and I would be rejoicing that my life has been productive and pleasing to the Lord.

The word of God cautions us to be as the wise and not as the unwise and making the best use of our time knowing the will of the Lord (Ephesians 5:15-17). When we sit and allow life to pass us by and not take action when needed, we will not reap because we have not sown (Ephesians 11:4). On the contrary, when we are continually productive, motivated and disciplined about life, daily, we become diligent and create room for God to trust us with more. Being a good steward of our time is honoring the one who gave it to use. Proverbs 3:4 speaks of the soul of the sluggard being in want and not receiving, but the soul of the diligent, hard-working is made fat.

God is very practical at times and non-complicated. When we begin to pay attention and study the character of God, we realize He is not only orderly but diligent, "hard-working," kempt, focused, has one mind (not wayward), disciplined, determined, fruitful, progressing, joyful and so much more. God produces fruits! That is what we ought to possess. Are you procrastinating about going back to school? What about leaving that job the Lord has been speaking to you about, cleaning your home, going to the doctor, reading the word, praying or fasting? Whatever it is, the Lord is concerned about every area of our lives and is calling us to action. He wants to bless us, but we also need to prove ourselves worthy of the weight of responsibility. Procrastination robs us of our now blessings and clutters our mind, spiritual life and natural space. Make room for God to walk and run freely in your life today.

Prayer

Lord Jesus, I thank You for being a God of order and progress. Lord, I desire Your character of ambition and hard work, for by being diligent, shall I rule in many nations and areas of my life. Set a fire of movement in my life this day and let my life never be stagnant but continue bearing fruits. In Jesus' mighty name, amen!!

My Declaration

My Delight!

Jesus, You are more than enough. You are more than words can describe. When our hearts delight in the Lord, He delights in us. The word delight means "please someone greatly or great pleasure." It also means "a strong feeling of happiness or satisfaction." So, when we have great pleasure, satisfaction and happiness in the Lord and the life He promises us, we grow in strength and in faith; we tend to relax more in Christ.

Great joy our Lord has for us when we trust Him fully. Have you ever been driving, and your neighbor isn't paying attention to their side of the road and swerves in your lane? Now, think about how often that has happened and how many more near-misses you had. That is reason to rejoice, have great pleasure or delight in the Lord, for He is the Great Protector!

I have, many times within a week's timeframe, come close to crashing or being ran into by my neighbors who are not paying attention. Imagine the number of unnecessary battles we did not have to fight, and the necessary peace we got instead! All the more reason to rejoice and delight in the Lord

I know God loves us and wants our timed life here on earth to be beautiful and filled with prosperity of mind, soul, and spirit, for He is a good, good Father! Amen!!!

My Declaration

Psalm 23:5

Thou preparest a table before me in the presence of mine enemies: thou anointest my head with oil. My cup runneth over. KJV

You prepare a table before me in the presence of my enemies. You have anointed and refreshed my head with oil. My cup overflows. AMP

You serve me a six-course dinner right in front of my enemies. You revive my drooping head. My cup brims with blessing. MSG

As you read these three powerful versions of Psalms 23:5, think on this. What would be the reason for our enemy and us to be seated at the same table, working on the same project, sitting next to each other or working at the same office? It is for God to show off on us.

The MSG said, "You lift my drooping head." When faced with hatred, anger or bitterness from those we loved, respect or know nothing about, God wants us to remain reliant on Him, knowing that He will personally put our enemies to shame. He will purposefully lavish you in their company. He will cause an impossible promotion to be yours; He will cause things you didn't work for or deserve to come chasing you down…why? Because you relied on His word and promises.

God will always confound the enemy in our lives once He is the source of our joy and the object of our faith. Our battles are not meant to destroy us, but to strengthen us and allow God to brag on what He has placed in us. When we raise our anointed head and walk boldly and joyfully amongst or enemies, it heaps coals of fire on their heads (Prov 25:21-22). Our responsibility is to pray, love our enemies and God's responsibility is to protect, provide for and torment the adversary against our lives by continually blessing us. Rejoice!! For this season, you have the upper hand!

Prayer

Heavenly Father, I thank You for today and I thank You for my life. I thank You for my six-course meal in the presence of my enemies. I thank You for the multiplication of blessings that will cause my adversaries to go mad in their failures, as they see You blessing me. For to You is all the glory, GREAT things you have done! In Jesus' name, amen!

My Declaration

_____
_____
_____
_____
_____
_____
_____
_____
_____
_____
_____
_____
_____
_____
_____
_____
_____
_____
_____
_____
_____
_____
_____
_____
_____
_____
_____
_____
_____
_____
_____

Seasons

In the very tempest of storms, He watches over us. Do you ever take note that all seasons are temporary? (Ecclesiastes 3:1-2) We often go through rough seasons and swear up and down that it is permanent, but it always ends. Winter, spring, summer and fall happens every year and the cycle never takes a vacation. So are the seasons in our own lives; surplus, wilderness, night, day, prosperity or whatever names we have for them. They, too, are in cycles. But one thing is certain, the one thing that doesn't change is God's consistent faithfulness to us in every season we face. So, whether we are on cloud nine or on ground zero, there is always a time of shifting and sifting.

It is for us to know what season we are in, learn what God wants us to do and transition on time to the next season. Enjoy the season you are in today, whether wilderness or promised land, because God does want to increase you in something. You may know what it is, but if you don't, ask Him, He will tell you for this is the best season for transformation and increase in wisdom. And if you are in a season of surplus, much is required of you, for to whom much is given much is required (Luke 12:48). A season of surplus requires a season of giving and sowing, whether in time, finances, advice or some other form of giving. You plant in this season to reap in the next.

Prayer

Lord Jesus, help me to discern the season I am in and to learn what valuable purpose I need to take from it. Father, whether the season is high or low, help me to be grateful that You are working on me and in me. In Jesus' name, amen.

My Declaration

Still Small Voice

Our God is so big, huge and powerful, yet He still chooses to speak in a still small voice. When Elijah ran away from Jezebel unto Horeb, the Lord could've spoken in the wind, earthquake or the fire, but He chooses to be present with a gentle whisper (1 Kings 19:1-12). In our modern society, the big, rich and wealthy are often seen and heard, but humility is frowned upon as weak. For a God like ours to give such an example is profound and needs to be taken note of.

In the Bible, we read our Lord was described as having no comeliness, no beauty that we should desire Him and rejected of men (Isaiah 53:2-3). Now, why would a God who owns it all not flaunt it all? Why would He send a Son that either looked like regular folks in His time or less than? He came clothed in humility and not pompously filled with distractions…...on purpose!

When we look at the character of Christ, it's nothing we see daily. We are often challenged to prove ourselves and sometimes dismissed because we proclaim a name but not flaunting possessions. But think about that still small voice. It is the one that has nothing to prove, but everything to give. It's the one who has the power to extinguish the world for its sinful nature but decides to have compassion and mercy. Such love!!

Prayer

Father, I thank You for Your still small voice. I thank You that I do not need to wait for a thunderous roar but to be still and listen for a gentle whisper. Lord, I ask You to tune my ears to Your still small voice. I ask that You change my character to match Yours and wash my confidence and strength in Yours authentically, so that I may walk in the authority You have given me. For Lord, it is only by Your grace, I can accomplish these things and be a sheep that knows Your voice. In Jesus' precious name I pray, amen!

My Declaration

_____
_____
_____
_____
_____
_____
_____
_____
_____
_____
_____
_____
_____
_____
_____
_____
_____
_____
_____
_____
_____
_____
_____
_____
_____
_____
_____
_____
_____

Thank God for Tomorrow

I thank you, Lord, that the enemies I see today, I shall see no more (Exodus 14:13).

The Lord has been most gracious and faithful towards us, His children. He allowed Himself to witness our disdainful and atrocious behaviors when we would run from Him, but His love remained, for He knew tomorrow would come with immense change.

Our greatest shame and our deepest darkest secrets are all light before our Father. We can come to Him and be transparent, and yet His love and welcoming arms will never fall away from us. When we are battling the darkness and the raging winds, thank God for tomorrow for it will come. When your life seems done, broken and facing "foreclosure," thank God for tomorrow. When the struggles of life come to call you defeated, remember all His promises and benefits towards you.

Tomorrow is God's word, manifested. It is God's promises come to life, walking, breathing, happening. Tomorrow is where we let go of the spirit of heaviness for the garment of praise. Tomorrow is where we hold God accountable and He proves Himself mighty. Tomorrow is where we can no longer walk in fear or defeat because the wisdom of today and yesterday taught us. Tomorrow is where we cross into our promise land and relish in the breathing, life-producing promises.

Prayer

Lord, I thank You for tomorrow. I thank You for manifestation, increase in faith and breakthroughs. I thank You for enlarging my territory and making my feet trod on dry land. Lord, I thank You for sustaining my today so that tomorrow I can behold Your glory. My life is in Your hands. In Jesus' name, amen.

My Declaration

_____
_____
_____
_____
_____
_____
_____
_____
_____
_____
_____
_____
_____
_____
_____
_____
_____
_____
_____
_____
_____
_____
_____
_____
_____
_____
_____
_____

She Left Her Waterpot

When Christ traveled to Samaria, He knew who He would meet and what the person He met would do for God's kingdom. We all know the story about the Woman of Samaria, some even know songs created about her. This story showed a Savior journeying specifically to correct a generation of wrong decisions in an individual's life, that would bless those around her and from her. In John 4:16, Jesus asked the woman to call her husband when she desired to learn more about the living water. The woman responded in honesty and Jesus confirmed. This had me thinking, when the Holy Spirit reveals to us our sins, our wrongs, our shortcomings, do we, as this woman, "own up to it" with a repentant heart or do we become defensive and continue in the lie?

When Christ confirmed, "Yes, you have five husbands and the one you are with now is not your own." (John 4:18) She could've lied, asked what He was talking about and missed the already building grace eruption in her life. Thankfully, she used wisdom. After all, she was in the presence of the Great Teacher, and was honest. The woman of Samaria experienced liberty in Christ's presence. Not only was she shocked a Jew asked her for water, but she was also even more stunned by his warm, soft-spoken, trustworthy demeanor. Because of what transpired in this intimate conversation, the woman forgot what her intentions were about the well.

When Christ reveals our sins to us, oftentimes they are not chewable or even able to be swallowed. We oftentimes feel regret, condemnation and want to hide away. By doing and allowing these thoughts, feelings and emotions, we rob ourselves of the already building grace eruption within our lives. We don't get to enjoy the amazing grace that our Lord and Savior Jesus Christ has afforded us.

I implore each of us today to live in the grace of God, allow Him to show us the unkind nature, lustful desires and uncanny ways we sometimes have. The Father chastens who He loves (Hebrews 12:6, Proverbs 3:12), because He is a good Father. Let us relax repentant on His love knowing that He reveals to us, so He can redeem us (1 Corinthians 2:10-12). So He can use us as He did with the woman of Samaria. Continue reading John 4 to see how this woman soaked up the grace of God and walked in liberty, knowing she was forgiven.

Prayer

Heavenly Father, I thank You that You are not a chastiser, but You are a father and a God of love and redemption. Father, every sin You have shown me up until now, I repent of them and I receive Your grace abounding in my life. I now chose to walk in liberty, letting others know unashamedly of Your redeeming power. Father, as You continue to reveal things in me that are not of Your kingdom, I ask for an appetite of repentance and for Your truth. I pray that all guilt, feelings of condemnation and shame be removed from my life now in Jesus' name! For I am a son/daughter of the Most High and once again, Father, You chasten those You love, and I am loved by You greatly. In Jesus' name, amen.

My Declaration

_____
_____
_____
_____
_____
_____
_____
_____
_____
_____
_____
_____
_____
_____
_____
_____
_____
_____
_____
_____
_____
_____
_____
_____
_____
_____

I That Speak Unto Thee Am He

As we continue from John 4:18, I want us to focus today on verse 26. After the woman of Samaria made a statement to our Lord that the "Messiah cometh, which is called Christ: when He is come, He will tell us all things" (v. 25), *His response was "I that speak unto thee am He"* (v. 26). I can imagine the stunned expression on her face, the increase in her heartbeat of extreme shock knowing that she was indeed in the presence of the Lord Jesus Christ. For a time, she anticipated this moment, and now it is here!
The presence of God is daily filled with room for us to join Him. He seeks us out because, too often, we are not seeking Him. What do you think your reaction would be if Jesus was sitting by you today? How would you approach the conversation? What would you ask? What all would you want to know? After you have answered these questions, take note that the omnipresent God is already sitting by you.

We often sing a song in church that "I'm chasing after you, no matter what I have to do, I need you more and more." Are we really the chaser or the chased? In the word of God, we see Jesus seeking out souls to save, heal, minister to, deliver or to just love on. We see Him calling the burdened to come unto Him, so He can provide rest (Matthew 11:28). We see Him freely giving away compassion, love and tender mercies (Jeremiah 29:11), even today.

All Of My Life
Devotional

Christ daily awaits our "chasing" after Him. He asks us to seek Him first (Matthew 6:33), not because He is being proud or laid back but because He wants our heartfelt intentions, not our obligations or lip services. He wants our heart; fully.

So, when the I Am is sitting next to us, He daily awaits our questions, cares, conversations and feedback to His provisions. I that speak am He; the woman knew that without Him, she could not, and with Him, she could. She had no reason to do, before His arrival.

Prior, we discussed how moved she was that the Messiah took time for her, He went specifically for her at that hour to not only correct a wrong, but to bring about purpose. A purpose she would not have known existed in her if it wasn't for Christ. Saints, in His presence, there is indeed fullness of joy and at His right hands' pleasures forevermore (Psalm 16:11b).

I that speak am He.... such an encounter! He is awaiting you today. Tell Him what is on your mind then listen intently for His response. The greatest love of all has chased you down and desires to keep you. We are never too far from Him to find us and wrap His loving arms around us. Whatever you are facing in this season, Jesus is speaking to you so you can heal, be delivered and propel you deeper into your purpose. The woman of Samaria expected condemnation from a Jew. She didn't get it. She expected rebuke from the Messiah. She received compassion and love, then she went on to change her entire "world" and those in it. Such love!

Prayer

Heavenly Father, most gracious God, omnipresent Father and most righteous Creator. I thank You for today, a day of purpose and I thank You for my life. Father, I thank You for the journey of life You have taken with me and I thank You for never giving up on me, even though I deserved it at times. Father God, I release my purpose, destiny and next steps into Your hands. May they be perfected in You and lead me in the paths of righteousness for Your namesake. Lord, I am covered by You, I am sought after by You and most importantly, I am loved by You. Let Your will be done and Your kingdom come in my life, this day, in Jesus' mighty name, amen

My Declaration

_____

_____

_____

_____

_____

_____

_____

_____

_____

_____

_____

_____

_____

_____

_____

_____

_____

_____

_____

_____

_____

_____

_____

_____

_____

_____

_____

_____

_____

_____

Stand!

When it seems, no one cares and the world is against you, He is in the midst of it gently carrying you along. I presume we've all seen the picture of footprints and the song "one set of footprints in the sand." God's promise still stands! He truly never leaves nor forsakes us. He is diligent and determined to see us cross the finish line of this life. When we deeply think of our Savior, we realize He is not limited by our laws and rules, but rather utilizes these laws and rules at times to benefit His kingdom. When we get to the full understanding and realization that we are all created to worship and serve Him in Spirit and truth (John 4:24), we can love Him deeply and know that all things are truly possible with God.

Sometimes we get caught up in the cliché of life's mantras where the word of God no longer comes with conviction. We say the joy of the Lord is my strength, but it's empty, no zeal, no conviction----a declaration of praise that our Lord will never receive. It's like a prayer prayed without faith or expectation (James 1:6-7). But my brothers and sisters, let us run and not be weary. Let us continue to fight the good fight of faith by implementing and living the practicality of the word of God in our daily lives.
Our adversary wants us to believe that there is no more to Christ and that we will not win. But pronounce him to be the liar that he is today and declare your worth in Christ. Declare your expected end, your prosperity here on earth and your ultimate destiny! Only you can live it as God intended.

Prayer

Lord, I thank You for calling me blessed. I thank You for calling me prosperous and sealing my destiny in Your hand. Lord, I declare today that I am who You say I am. I declare that any stagnation in my life, I chose to believe, by faith is ended, now! I believe and declare that all You created me for will be accomplished in my life here on earth. You are the Lord and Savior over my life, In Jesus' precious name I pray, amen!

My Declaration

_____
_____
_____
_____
_____
_____
_____
_____
_____
_____
_____
_____
_____
_____
_____
_____
_____
_____
_____
_____
_____
_____
_____
_____
_____
_____
_____
_____

The Wait

Fred Hammond sings a scripture found in Isaiah 40:31, which states: "But they that wait upon the Lord shall renew their strength; they shall mount up with wings as eagles; they shall run, and not be weary; and they shall walk, and not faint. KJV

This scripture is that of growth and progress in the Lord. Many times, God gives us a word through visions and dreams, while we are praying or through another person in the body of Christ and we become very excited. Through this excitement, we may move too quickly. Sometimes when we get a word we have been longing for, for so long, we take matters into our own hands thinking the timing is now and that God needs our help *hides face* sounds familiar? I believe we all have been there some time in our lives. Some are there right now, but do not worry. He is always patient with us.

You see beloved, God oftentimes uses these opportunities of waiting to teach us temperance and patience. I know this was never a strong ability of mine, but with time I'm getting better and so will you. Isaiah 40:31 denotes that while we wait, we increase in strength (spiritual), but how? Another promise the Lord made is that found in Nehemiah 8:10c (the joy of the Lord is our strength) and we find that joy in Psalm 16:11 (…in your presence there is fullness of joy…AMP). So, in the wait, we receive strength, which stems from joy, which comes from faith and trust in God. So, we should be in the presence of the Lord during the wait!!

If we focus on these scriptures and others such as Philippians 4:13, we realize that waiting on God releases us from worry, fret, stress, impulsivity, and impatience. Waiting builds us in character, increases our faith and trust in God and allows us to be led faithfully by God into the manifestation. I know, I know, waiting on God's "soon" can be 21 days, 21 months or even 21 years.

So, what do we do while we are waiting on the manifestation of His promises? We preoccupy ourselves with seeking Him, get to know Him more, get to know who you are in Him, more, walk in your purpose and ask for patience during the wait. To faithfully wait comes with some great benefits; we are increasing in the spirit (eagle), we gain strength in mind and spirit and we become steadfast, unmovable and filled with temperance and faith in God. We become more like Christ. Isn't that ironically amazing! Through all the strenuous times we must wait, God is teaching us to be more like Christ.

The wait isn't meant to weigh us down but to build us in the Spirit and in the knowledge of Christ.

Prayer

Lord Jesus, I thank You for the many lessons I am taught in this class of life. Lord, I truly ask You today to teach me how to not allow the weight of the wait to discourage or tear me down. Lord, I ask You for strength according to Your Word, that will allow me to faithfully wait on Your timing and not intervene.

I can't do this on my own, Lord. Lord Jesus, I repent this day for meddling with Your process and I take my hands off that situation. Lord Jesus, as You have Your way in my life, I will rejoice in temperance, I will grow in trust and I will increase in my faith in You. Lord, I also thank You for the manifestation in advance of Your promises towards me. Your will be done. Your kingdom come, in Jesus' mighty name, amen!!

My Declaration

_____
_____
_____
_____
_____
_____
_____
_____
_____
_____
_____
_____
_____
_____
_____
_____
_____
_____
_____
_____
_____
_____
_____
_____

Trusting God
A Man After God's Own Heart

When we read throughout the Book of Psalms, one would conclude that Psalmist David had some serious issues. One moment he is exalting and worshipping God, but the next, he is broken, hurting and praying for the destruction and demise of his enemies.

Just like David, we've all experienced some form of hurt or lack, but what do we do with it? David cried out to God, *"I am weary with my groaning; all the night make I my bed to swim; I water my couch with my tears. 7 Mine eye is consumed because of grief; it waxeth old because of all mine enemies." (Psalm 6:6-7)*

Although David would present himself naked before God in his troubles, he did something even greater; he trusted God and worshipped Him in his dire circumstances. David rejoiced in the good, the bad, the ugly and the disgusting.

It's very easy to praise and worship God in the good times, when our finances are enough, our relationships are going right across the board, and our health is intact. David knew this. I truly believe throughout his life, David had to make/force himself to rejoice in adversities until it became natural. David was also in love with his Savior and experienced the Holy Spirit in a time where relationship was not commonplace. David pursued God in all things, he sought God's heart and answers; and continually strove to do the will of God.

Trusting isn't always easy, but when we decide in our minds to trust God, our living begins to make sense. Our situations begin to look easier and we even obtain wisdom because why? We have now released our fears to Him.

Prayer

Father, I thank You for making me in Your image and likeness. Thank You, Lord, for teaching me how to seek after Your heart in this season. Father, You have said You seek such that will worship You in Spirit and in truth, and as David used what he had, I will use what You have given me, Your Spirit, and seek after Your heart. Father, I release all my fears to You this day and I chose to trust You with all of me, withholding nothing. Your kingdom come and Your will be done in my life, in Jesus' name, amen!

My Declaration

_____
_____
_____
_____
_____
_____
_____
_____
_____
_____
_____
_____
_____
_____
_____
_____
_____
_____
_____
_____
_____
_____
_____
_____
_____

Value Your Time

Prudent means "acting with or showing care and thought for the future." So, this means time is carefully planned. Think of it as a weekly or monthly budget where every penny has a purpose- every second has a purpose. Idleness kills, just as procrastination kills. When time is used wisely each day, your soul will be fulfilled. You will end each day feeling accomplished and ready to do better tomorrow. Ephesians 5:15-17 warns about living wisely and making the most of our time as the days are evil. Wisdom says steward our 24 hours, plan them out not just with our natural duties, but with our Kingdom duties as well.

Wisdom says to live a disciplined life where our time is stewarded with the help of the Holy Spirit; after all, He is the great helper. Our 24-hour days will not increase to 30, 40 or even 50, for God knew it was all we needed to either be productive or fail.

Think of where you desire to be in this life, then look at your time management currently. Will God give you more responsibilities seeing how you handle your time presently? Or will He hold off or give your 1 talent to another. Make the best of your time today. Charles Spurgeon wrote, "Serve God by doing common (daily) actions in a heavenly spirit (as unto God), and then, if your daily calling only leaves you cracks and crevices of time, fill them up with holy service."

Proverbs 6:6-8; Proverbs 21:5; Psalm 55:16-17; Proverbs 14:23r; Proverbs 20:13; Proverbs 6:9; Proverbs 10:6; Ecclessiastes 3:1-2; John 9:4; Colossians 4

We spend so much time daily that its value isn't thought about. Time has become second nature and not at the forefront of our minds as with our other important things in life. Many of us use time wisely, as a prudent man should, and God blesses us with fields of production and prosperity. Whether it is book publishing, large seminars/conference, promotions or simply having the ability to spend quality time with family or resting. When we waste time, that is allowing it to go by without purposefully utilizing it. We mismanage a precious gift from God while the enemy cheers us on. Remember, our days are numbered and but a few.

We all, rich and poor, have a designated 24-hours in a day, but the rich man seems to be making the most of it. What is the poor man doing with his time that he cannot become the rich man? He is possibly wasting away watching TV, scrolling through social media, video games or laying lazily around waiting for angels to chauffeur him. Let us be diligent and steward this wonderful gift called time our Father has bestowed upon us. Let us honor Him daily with great stewardship with Him by our side.

Prayer

Lord Jesus, You are the author and finisher of our faith. From creation, You showed us how to be good stewards as You created and rested on the seventh day. Your rest was an act of wisdom. Lord, I repent for mismanagement and filling my time with ludicrous and empty tasks that did not benefit my purpose. I ask You to help me become all You have created me to be and to manage each second, minute and hour in Your wisdom. I accept Your forgiveness and I give You full control to lead my life. In Jesus' name, amen!

My Declaration

Why not me?

In this process of life, we go through trials, tribulations, persecutions, pains, emotional rollercoasters, regret, hurt and many more negative situations. We are even faced with some hard hurts, mostly from those we hold very close. During the fire is when our heart begins to really show.

Oftentimes we get upset, our attitude dulls or rages, and we get upset with God. We blare the following questions like a loudspeaker in an empty stadium "why me God?", "Why must I go through this?" and the most common "When will this end?"

Some troubles last days, weeks, months, and when God really wants to get our attention and break our selfish, entitled ways, He will keep us in the fire for even years. Amidst all these questions, the one we so seldom ask is "Why not me?" or "Why should I not suffer for righteousness sake?", "Why should I not "sell" my earthly possessions and take up my cross and follow God?" "Why not me?"

Apostle Paul was imprisoned for quite some time. He could not freely go and he could not freely come. He was used to his freedom, going where the Spirit of God led him to preach the gospel, but....now.....he's in chains and guarded 24/7. He is away from his family, mentees, friends, church and home. Through suffering these afflictions, he rejoiced nonetheless (Read Philippians 4).

Apostle Paul counted his prison sentence as joy to suffer for Christ. He rejoiced in his light afflictions, looking onward to the greater reward that lies ahead (Philippians 4:11, 13); (2 Corinthians 4:17). He knew his suffering was temporary, necessary and without a shadow of a doubt, knew it would always work out for his good (Romans 8:28).

Whatever battle, disappointment, hurt, loss, pain or anguish you are experiencing today, for the sake of Christ or you may have brought it on yourself, is it for the betterment of your soul?

Ask yourself these questions:
-- "Why not me?"
-- "Why not my life to be used as an example to bless someone else's, to draw someone to Christ?"

We are not greater than our master (John 3:16), Jesus Christ, who suffered much for our sake BEFORE He got to the cross. Though painful, it is a privilege and an honor when God trusts us to test us. He has already proclaimed us as His royal priesthood, who are made in His image and loved by Him.

Prayer

Lord Jesus, I thank You for opening my eyes to see the beauty within the ashes of my hurt, my regrets, and my disappointments. Father, as You sent Your Son to suffer viciously for me, which He did obediently unto death, I ask You for that same strength through these trying times. Lord Jesus, I forgive all those who have hurt me, abandoned me, rejected me, spoken evil of me and Lord, I also ask for Your forgiveness for those whom I have hurt, chastised, mocked, rejected and abandoned. I release it all to You and I boldly make this statement, "Why not me?" Holy Spirit, I ask You to help me to be the unique person You have called me to be and with Your strength and guidance, I will do nothing but rise in victory. I thank You for Your forgiveness, in Jesus' name I pray, amen.

P.S. encourage someone today (Philippians 4:19)

My Declaration

What Do You Have To Show For Yourself?

This question or rather accusation has crossed the mind of every human being. We reach stages or seasons where we look back and wonder where has the time gone and what did we do with our childhood dreams or life. We have dreams of becoming lawyers, doctors, astronaut's and some children just want to be mommy or daddy. But whatever the innocence produced, when we increase in age, we are oftentimes disappointed. That's not the job I wanted! That's not the home I wanted! Or, this is not how I saw my life! But I have this one question beloved, when did you draft the transcript for your life? Do we go to God to see what He has already planned? Okay, it was two questions.

I know for myself it took some tears, anguish and disappointments before I asked God or yelled rather, "WHAT DO YOU WANT FROM ME" and He responded calmly and lovingly, "For you to seek my face and do my will." Needless to say, I didn't want to hear that. I wanted a specific answer. I wanted the clouds to open and a big sign in the sky to say "go there..., do this... and you'll accomplish this..." But our Father does not work that way. He wants us to seek Him not because we want something but because we want Him.

So, what do you have to show for yourself? Did you lose your dream or did God lead you to another path? Have you lost hope because you are now a certain age and do not have the wealth, spouse or children in your timeline? One of the many things I admire about God is that although He loves us dearly, He isn't moved by our emotions or tantrums. Concerned yes, but not moved. He knows best at all times. Can a pot tell its maker how to create it? Can a man tell God, His Creator, how to lead his life? Who would be God and who would be Creator? I encourage you all reading this today to give your life, all of it to God. Not just Sundays or when trouble comes but give Him everything concerning you. Let go of all timetables and disappointments.

God does not make mistakes, and you are not going to have Him start making them. Our lives are a gift and treasure carefully put together by the Master and carefully protected and guided, if we allow this. Know that every disappointment is for God and once you know of a certainty that you have given your life completely and utterly to God, nothing withholding, then you'll know that even when you feel like a failure, God is behind the scenes making you a winner. Trust Him to lead. A man's heart plans his way, but God directs his steps (Proverbs 16:9). Won't you trust Him today?

Prayer

Lord Jesus, I thank You for my life. Yes, it's not what I thought it would be, but it's exactly what You wanted it to be. I thank You for my purpose, my transitions and all my disappointments and failures that have brought me to this point. They have and will continue to work for my good! Lord, I trust You. Lord, I know You will lead me in the paths of righteousness and Your righteous will never be put to shame. Lord, You care about my career, my family life, relationships, ministries and all things concerning me, so I release it all to You today, knowing that You will make all things great in Your timing. Lord, help me to continue to trust You even in dark tunnels when my eyes are blinded and help me to rely on You when I'm at crossroads. These things I pray, in Jesus' name, amen!

My Declaration

_____
_____
_____
_____
_____
_____
_____
_____
_____
_____
_____
_____
_____
_____
_____
_____
_____
_____
_____
_____
_____
_____
_____
_____
_____
_____
_____
_____
_____

Walk in Purpose

"What is necessary isn't always beneficial." Oftentimes we take on tasks that we deem necessary or important, but it does not produce any real fruit. It may give us quick self-gratification but does not last for a long time.

God is a God of purpose and whatsoever He does or asks us to do produces fruits that are long-lasting, sustainable and springs forth increase in our lives and those around us. When we go to make a decision, we normally focus on the "right now" benefit and not the long-term. God has designed our purpose to be sustainable and always producing.

When Esther went on a mission to King Ahasuerus, she was possibly thinking about how to free her people in that era, but not the positive consequences it will have for years to come. She knew what she had to do, which was necessary, and she knew it was beneficial to herself, a kingdom and her people. And God worked it in all their favor.

When we look at the life of Jesus Christ, we notice what everything He did on earth was for a purpose, to produce more fruits and it was always intentional. The healing of the blind and casting out of devils was not so He could get accolades or self-gratification in the moment. It was to produce long-life benefits to his children, such as knowing our authority and know that God can indeed do the impossible.

Now that we have entered a new year of the Supernatural, the intentionality of our actions are more needed than ever. The purpose behind it is even more important. Will that job benefit the purpose God has placed you here for? Will buying that house in this season allow you to reap the benefits for years to come or will the rewards die quickly? Will any decision you are making now be beneficial for the Kingdom of God in your life or will it be self-gratifying until the "happy" dies out of it.

Let us be purpose minded and purpose-driven. Our Father desires for us to be full, in good health and to prosper as our soul prospers (3 John 2:2). We should leave this earth on empty because we have fulfilled all that God placed us here to do. That should be our conviction.

Prayer

Heavenly Father, You have shown time and time again that You're a God of purpose. Lord, I ask You to keep me within Your will and teach me to know my purpose that I may walk within it at all times. Give me wisdom on the career, home, spouse, business deals, business ideas and/or field You want me to major in. I desire to produce fruits all the days of my life in Your will. Increase my capacity in the spirit of wisdom, knowledge and understanding that I may do Your will on purpose and to know that although a thing may be necessary, it may not be beneficial to my purpose or destiny. In Jesus' name, amen!

My Declaration

You Are Destined To Overcome

You are built to last as a kingdom citizen. With Christ's approval on your life, you are meant to rule, reign and dominate in the natural realm and in the spiritual realm. You ARE made to conquer!

The scripture says, "I can do all things through Christ who strengthens me" (Philippians 4:13) is to be taken in a literal sense. If God has led you to do the most difficult task in our lives, REJOICE for this is a time for His word to come manifestly to you. Sometimes, when we are faced with challenges, we grow weak, timid and fearful, but rest assured beloved, as the Lord brings you to it, He is faithful to bring you all the way through it.

The manuscript for your life, as we all know, was written before our existence. Think on this. If that be true (and it is), can we, as true believers, fail? If the one and only true living God has set our course, placed in certain obstacles, rigged the obstacles so that we always come out winning in wisdom, strength, increased faith and patience in Him, and provoke a hunger for righteousness, how can we lose! We ARE overcomers.

Our father makes no mistakes. Whatever you are facing today, God makes no mistakes. It will ALWAYS work out for your good! Just remain faithful in the things of God, continue to be a son/daughter of the King, continue to rest in Him…...He is your Daddy and desires for your soul to prosper! So, PROSPER beloved, in all things PROSPER! In your soul, prosper! In your mind, prosper! In your relationships, PROSPER! In your emotions, PROSPER! In your finances, PROSPER! In your God-given careers, PROSPER! In your destiny, PROPER! In your purpose, PROSPER! (1 John 5:4-5).

Prayer

Lord Jesus, I now step into overcomer status, for You have not created me cursed but blessed. Lord, I thank You for my identity in You as a Kingdom citizen that is made to overcome, that is made to prosper. Father, I do declare that in ALL things from this day forward, I will prosper. I declare that whatever opportunities I have lost because I did not know my full identity in You as a Kingdom citizen is restored, I declare I am more than a conquer in You. I declare I will prosper as my soul prospers. I declare I will hunger for You more. I declare I will know You more. I declare I will obtain all territories belonging to me in the natural realm and the spiritual realm. I declare every spiritual womb that has been shut is opened now! I declare my royal priestly status shall begin to manifest, In Jesus' mighty name, amen!!

My Declaration

_____
_____
_____
_____
_____
_____
_____
_____
_____
_____
_____
_____
_____
_____
_____
_____
_____
_____
_____
_____
_____
_____
_____
_____
_____
_____
_____
_____

You Have Been Promoted

When we hear the word promotion, we become excited and become expectant of what the Lord will do. Promotion is a noun which means to support or provide active encouragement for the furtherance of a cause or aim. It also means to publicize or to increase public awareness, advancement. In our world, one has to work to be promoted and sometimes we will get overlooked depending on who the competition is and what advantage they have.

In the Bible, we read about abundance, prosperity and all kinds of promotions. We see breakthroughs in those small black words on white paper, both in the natural and spiritual realm. We see men and women of God walking and living in victories, some of us only dream of. It then becomes easy, within human nature to think back in the Bible era, that it was easier than this century. What would you think if I was to say life now, in this era, is easier? Hopefully, you would smile and concur.

Today a broken spirit and contrite heart God will not despise (Psalm 51:17). With a sincere, penitent heart, He meets you right where you are. I believe one of the best places to be in life is low, in every sense of the word. Low in spirit, low in demeanor, low in mind, even low and downtrodden. Now, what in the world is this person talking about, you say? This is where God can get the full glory out of our lives, strip us of the fleshly nature and then promote us to bigger and greater things in Him. Remember Job? How about David?

All Of My Life
Devotional

I remember a time in my life when everything I was made
of emotionally and mentally was drained. Tears were no
longer affordable for I was bankrupt, all cried out. I became
numb; nothing mattered anymore. Little did I know that
was exactly where God wanted me to be. He wanted me at
my wit's end where my flesh failed, my own intellect
became foolish and my height of education or salary could
not save me. That's when He said, "I had to take you low,
to build you up." Then came my supernatural promotion,
soundness of mind, vitality in life, peace, favor of God and
many blessings.

Allow the Lord to complete His work in you this season
and you will live the promoted life. Allow Him to be your
yes and no. Allow Him to be in your next decisions. Allow
Him to be and do what He is perfect at being God!

Prayer

Lord Jesus, I thank You for Your promotion in every area
of my life. Lord, as I become low so that You can build me
up, I decrease so that You may increase in the lives of
myself, my family and anyone I come in contact with. My
life belongs to You for You give and take away, and this
life You decided to give. I release all my personal wealth,
accolades, way of thinking, to You. Lord have Your way.
In Jesus' name, amen.

My Declaration

_____
_____
_____
_____
_____
_____
_____
_____
_____
_____
_____
_____
_____
_____
_____
_____
_____
_____
_____
_____
_____
_____
_____
_____
_____
_____

Love Letter

Dear Lord,

The blood You shed was more than enough! The lashes and whips and broken skin You took for me were unmeasurable and incomparable, and I can't wrap my head around it. On purpose, You mentioned my name, proclaimed me worthy and suffered for my freedom. My freedom to live and move and have my being is in You. My freedom to live in the fullness of what God the Father wanted me to live in is in You. My freedom to be an inhabitant of the Holy Spirit is because of You. I do thank You and I just want to say, I love You, Lord. I know I don't say it much, but here goes….Now, You know I love You because You first loved me, but I love You because You not only tolerate me, but You adore me. You take the time each and every day to work with me and on me, unto perfection. You cherish me and call me Your own. I love You because you left me a great instrumental manual called the Bread of Life to guide me while You are physically absent but spiritually present. I love You because You have been a great supplier of needs. I love You because You give me the wisdom to meet all my wants. I love You because You gave me great health, even if it isn't fully manifested, by faith I know it is so. I love You because You hear all my prayers. I love You because You chose not to answer some. I love You because there is nothing I can do to turn Your love away from me or repay You. I love You because You first loved me.

Your greatest delight,
Your child

My Declaration

Contact Lorie-Ann today!

Email: umbrellaministries31@gmail.com